THE ART AND SCIENCE OF HOSPITAL MANAGEMENT

Chapters:

1. Introduction to Hospital Management
2. Historical Evolution of Healthcare Administration
3. The Role of a Hospital Manager
4. Strategic Planning in Healthcare
5. Financial Management in Hospitals
6. Human Resources Management
7. Quality and Patient Safety
8. Information Technology in Healthcare
9. Legal and Ethical Considerations
10. Crisis and Risk Management
11. Innovations in Healthcare Delivery
12. Community and Public Health Relations
13. Patient Experience and Satisfaction
14. Future Trends in Hospital Management
15. Case Studies and Best Practices

INTRODUCTION & CHAPTER SUMMARIES
THE ART AND SCIENCE OF HOSPITAL MANAGEMENT

The healthcare sector is one of the most dynamic and complex industries, continually evolving in response to scientific advancements, technological innovations, demographic shifts, and changing regulatory landscapes. At the heart of this sector is hospital management, a discipline that requires a delicate balance between art and science. Effective hospital management ensures that healthcare facilities operate smoothly, provide high-quality patient care, and remain financially viable.

Hospital management encompasses a wide range of responsibilities, from strategic planning and financial oversight to human resources management and patient safety. It requires a comprehensive understanding of healthcare systems, as well as the ability to lead multidisciplinary teams, make data-driven decisions, and navigate the intricate web of healthcare regulations and policies.

The Significance of Hospital Management

The importance of hospital management cannot be overstated. Hospitals are not just places where medical treatments are provided; they are complex organisations where numerous interconnected systems and processes work in tandem to deliver care. Effective management ensures that these systems function seamlessly, resources are utilised efficiently, and patients receive the best possible care.

In today's healthcare environment, hospital managers face numerous challenges, including rising operational costs, increasing patient expectations, regulatory pressures, and the need for continuous improvement. Addressing these challenges requires a deep understanding of both the macro and micro aspects of healthcare delivery, as well as the ability to implement innovative solutions that enhance efficiency and improve patient outcomes.

The Dual Nature of Hospital Management

Hospital management is both an art and a science. The scientific aspect involves the application of evidence-based practices, data analytics, and management theories to optimise hospital operations. It requires a thorough understanding of healthcare economics, quality management principles, and the use of information technology in healthcare.

On the other hand, the art of hospital management involves leadership, communication, and the ability to inspire and motivate teams. It requires empathy, emotional intelligence, and the ability to build strong relationships with staff, patients, and stakeholders. Successful hospital managers are those who can blend these two aspects effectively, creating an environment where clinical excellence and operational efficiency go hand in hand.

Objectives of This Book

This book aims to provide a comprehensive guide to hospital management, covering both the theoretical and practical aspects of the discipline. It is designed for current and aspiring hospital managers, healthcare administrators, and anyone interested in understanding the complexities of managing a healthcare facility.

The chapters that follow will delve into various aspects of hospital management, offering insights, strategies, and best practices. From strategic planning and financial management to patient safety and quality improvement, each chapter will provide valuable information that can be applied in real-world settings.

- **Chapter 1: Introduction to Hospital Management**
  This chapter provides an overview of hospital management, highlighting its importance and the key responsibilities of hospital managers.

- **Chapter 2: Historical Evolution of Healthcare Administration**
  A look at how healthcare administration has evolved over the years, from early hospitals to modern-day healthcare systems.

- **Chapter 3: The Role of a Hospital Manager**
  An in-depth examination of the various roles and responsibilities of a hospital manager, including leadership, strategic planning, and operational oversight.

- **Chapter 4: Strategic Planning in Healthcare**
  This chapter explores the importance of strategic planning in healthcare and provides a framework for developing effective strategies.

- **Chapter 5: Financial Management in Hospitals**
  An exploration of financial management principles, including budgeting, financial reporting, and cost control in hospitals.

- **Chapter 6: Human Resources Management**
  A look at the critical role of human resources in hospitals, covering recruitment, training, performance management, and employee relations.

- **Chapter 7: Quality and Patient Safety**
  This chapter focuses on quality management and patient safety, including the implementation of quality improvement initiatives and patient safety protocols.

- **Chapter 8: Information Technology in Healthcare**

An examination of the role of information technology in healthcare, including electronic health records, telemedicine, and health information systems.

- **Chapter 9: Legal and Ethical Considerations**
  A discussion of the legal and ethical issues that hospital managers must navigate, including healthcare laws, patient rights, and ethical dilemmas.

- **Chapter 10: Crisis and Risk Management**
  This chapter covers the principles of crisis and risk management, including emergency preparedness, risk assessment, and response strategies.

- **Chapter 11: Innovations in Healthcare Delivery**
  An exploration of the latest innovations in healthcare delivery, including new care models, technology-driven solutions, and patient-centred approaches.

- **Chapter 12: Community and Public Health Relations**
  A look at the role of hospitals in the community, including public health initiatives, community outreach, and partnerships with other organisations.

- **Chapter 13: Patient Experience and Satisfaction**
  This chapter examines the factors that influence patient experience and satisfaction, and strategies for improving them.

- **Chapter 14: Future Trends in Hospital Management**
  A forward-looking chapter that explores emerging trends and future challenges in hospital management.

- **Chapter 15: Case Studies and Best Practices**
  A collection of case studies and best practices from leading hospitals, providing practical examples of successful hospital management.

Conclusion

Hospital management is a multifaceted discipline that requires a combination of knowledge, skills, and personal attributes. By blending the art and science of management, hospital managers can ensure that their facilities deliver high-quality care, operate efficiently, and adapt to the ever-changing healthcare landscape. This book aims to equip readers with the tools and insights needed to excel in this challenging and rewarding field.

CHAPTER 1: INTRODUCTION TO HOSPITAL MANAGEMENT

Hospital management is a specialised field within healthcare administration that focuses on the effective operation of hospitals and healthcare facilities. It involves overseeing various departments, managing resources, ensuring compliance with regulations, and most importantly, providing a high standard of patient care. The role of a hospital manager is both challenging and rewarding, requiring a unique blend of leadership skills, healthcare knowledge, and administrative expertise.

The Core Functions of Hospital Management

Hospital management encompasses several core functions that are essential for the smooth operation of healthcare facilities:

1. **Leadership and Governance**: Hospital managers provide strategic direction and leadership to ensure that the hospital's mission, vision, and values are realised. This involves

setting goals, developing policies, and creating a culture of excellence and accountability.

2. **Operational Management**: This involves overseeing the day-to-day operations of the hospital, including patient admissions, staffing, facility maintenance, and service delivery. Effective operational management ensures that all departments function cohesively and efficiently.

3. **Financial Management**: Hospital managers are responsible for budgeting, financial planning, and resource allocation. They must ensure that the hospital remains financially viable while providing high-quality care. This includes managing revenue streams, controlling costs, and ensuring transparency in financial reporting.

4. **Human Resources Management**: The success of a hospital largely depends on its staff. Hospital managers must recruit, train, and retain skilled professionals, as well as manage employee relations and performance. Creating a supportive and motivating work environment is crucial for staff satisfaction and patient care.

5. **Quality and Patient Safety**: Ensuring the safety and well-being of patients is a primary concern. Hospital managers must implement quality assurance programs, monitor clinical outcomes, and promote a culture of continuous improvement. This includes adhering to regulatory standards and best practices in patient care.

6. **Compliance and Legal Issues**: Hospitals must comply with a myriad of regulations and laws. Hospital managers need to be well-versed in healthcare laws, accreditation standards, and ethical guidelines. They must ensure that the hospital operates within legal frameworks and maintains the highest ethical standards.

The Challenges of Hospital Management

Managing a hospital comes with numerous challenges, many of which are unique to the healthcare sector:

1. **Rising Costs**: Healthcare costs are continually rising due to factors such as technological advancements, an ageing population, and increased demand for services. Hospital managers must find ways to control costs without compromising on the quality of care.

2. **Regulatory Changes**: Healthcare is a highly regulated industry, and hospitals must constantly adapt to new laws and regulations. This requires staying informed about changes and implementing necessary adjustments promptly.

3. **Technological Advancements**: The rapid pace of technological change in healthcare presents both opportunities and challenges. Hospital managers must assess new technologies, integrate them into existing systems, and ensure that staff are adequately trained.

4. **Patient Expectations**: Patients today are more informed and have higher expectations regarding their care. Hospital managers must focus on improving patient satisfaction and experience, which involves enhancing communication, reducing wait times, and ensuring compassionate care.

5. **Workforce Management**: Recruiting and retaining skilled healthcare professionals is a significant challenge. Hospital managers must address issues such as staff burnout, continuing education, and creating a positive work environment to maintain a competent and motivated workforce.

The Skills and Qualities of an Effective Hospital Manager

Effective hospital managers possess a unique set of skills and qualities that enable them to navigate the complexities of healthcare management:

1. **Leadership Skills**: Strong leadership is essential for guiding teams, making strategic decisions, and fostering a positive organisational culture. Hospital managers must inspire confidence and lead by example.

2. **Communication Skills**: Effective communication is crucial for coordinating with staff, patients, and stakeholders. Hospital managers must be able to convey information clearly and listen actively to feedback and concerns.

3. **Analytical Skills**: Hospital managers must analyse data to make informed decisions. This includes financial analysis, performance metrics, and patient outcomes. Being able to interpret complex information is vital for strategic planning and problem-solving.

4. **Adaptability**: The healthcare environment is dynamic, and hospital managers must be adaptable to change. This involves being open to new ideas, learning continuously, and responding effectively to unexpected challenges.

5. **Empathy and Compassion**: Healthcare is inherently people-focused. Hospital managers must demonstrate empathy and compassion towards patients and staff, fostering an environment of care and respect.

6. **Problem-Solving Skills**: Hospitals face a wide range of challenges, from operational issues to patient care concerns. Hospital managers must be adept at identifying problems, developing solutions, and implementing changes effectively.

Conclusion

Hospital management is a critical and multifaceted discipline that requires a combination of leadership, strategic planning, and operational expertise. As the healthcare landscape continues to evolve, the role of hospital managers becomes increasingly important. By understanding the core functions, challenges, and required skills, current and aspiring hospital managers can better prepare themselves to lead healthcare facilities towards success.

In the chapters that follow, we will delve deeper into each aspect of hospital management, providing practical insights and strategies for effective leadership in healthcare. From financial management and quality assurance to human resources and patient experience, this book will serve as a comprehensive guide for anyone involved in the complex and rewarding field of hospital management.

CHAPTER 2: HISTORICAL EVOLUTION OF HEALTHCARE ADMINISTRATION

Healthcare administration has undergone significant transformation over the centuries, evolving from rudimentary management practices to the sophisticated systems we see today. Understanding this historical evolution provides valuable insights into how current practices have been shaped and highlights the continuous need for innovation and improvement in healthcare administration.

Early Beginnings

The roots of healthcare administration can be traced back to ancient civilisations, where rudimentary forms of medical care were provided in temples and other community centres. In ancient Egypt, for instance, priests often doubled as healers, and the management of healthcare was intertwined with religious practices. Similarly, in ancient Greece, temples dedicated to Asclepius, the god of medicine, served as centres for medical care, where priests managed both spiritual and physical healing.

During these early periods, the concept of specialised healthcare administration was virtually non-existent. Medical care was largely informal, provided by individuals who held multiple roles within their communities. The administration of healthcare was a communal effort, with no distinct managerial framework.

The Middle Ages

The Middle Ages saw the establishment of more formal healthcare institutions, particularly in the form of monastic hospitals. Monasteries became centres of medical knowledge and care, offering services to the sick and needy. These early hospitals were often funded by religious orders and charitable donations, and their management was overseen by monks and nuns.

The administration of these hospitals began to take on more structured forms. Monastic hospitals had specific roles for individuals responsible for various aspects of care and management, such as the almoner, who distributed alms and managed finances, and the infirmarian, who cared for the sick. This period marked the beginning of more organised approaches to healthcare administration, although it remained deeply intertwined with religious institutions.

The Renaissance and Enlightenment

The Renaissance and Enlightenment periods brought significant advancements in medical knowledge and practices, which in turn influenced healthcare administration. The establishment of universities and medical schools led to the professionalisation of medicine, with increased emphasis on education and scientific inquiry.

Hospitals became more secular during this time, and their administration began to reflect the growing complexity of medical care. The need for specialised management roles became apparent as hospitals expanded and the volume of patients increased. Administrative responsibilities such as record-keeping, financial management, and the coordination of medical staff became more distinct and formalised.

The 19th Century: The Birth of Modern Healthcare Administration

The 19th century marked a pivotal point in the evolution of healthcare administration, driven by the Industrial Revolution and significant public health challenges. Rapid urbanisation and the associated spread of diseases highlighted the need for better-organised healthcare systems.

Florence Nightingale's contributions during the Crimean War were instrumental in shaping modern healthcare administration. Her emphasis on sanitation, record-keeping, and hospital organisation laid the groundwork for systematic management practices. Nightingale's work demonstrated the importance of evidence-based management and the use of data to improve patient outcomes.

The establishment of public health institutions and the introduction of health insurance schemes also contributed to the development of healthcare administration. Governments began to play a more active role in health care, recognising the need for organised systems to manage public health issues and deliver medical services effectively.

The 20th Century: Professionalisation and Expansion

The 20th century saw the professionalisation of healthcare administration as a distinct field. The establishment of professional organisations, such as the American College of Healthcare Executives (ACHE) in 1933, underscored the importance of specialised training and professional standards for healthcare managers.

The post-World War II era brought significant changes, including the expansion of healthcare services, the introduction of new medical technologies, and the development of comprehensive healthcare systems. In many countries, the establishment of national health services and insurance schemes created complex administrative structures that required skilled management.

The role of hospital administrators evolved to encompass a wide range of responsibilities, including strategic planning, financial management, human resources, and quality assurance. The advent of health information technology in the latter part of the 20th century further transformed healthcare administration, enabling more efficient management of patient records, billing, and data analysis.

The 21st Century: Modern Challenges and Innovations

The 21st century has brought both challenges and innovations to healthcare administration. Advances in medical technology, an ageing population, and increasing healthcare costs have placed significant demands on healthcare managers. The globalisation of healthcare, with patients seeking care across borders, has added another layer of complexity.

One of the most significant developments in recent years has been the widespread adoption of electronic health records (EHRs) and other health information technologies. These technologies have revolutionised the way healthcare is managed, enabling better coordination of care, improved patient outcomes, and more efficient use of resources.

Healthcare administration today requires a balance of traditional management skills and a deep understanding of modern technologies. The focus on patient-centred care has also shifted the role of administrators towards ensuring that healthcare delivery is not only efficient but also compassionate and responsive to patients' needs.

Conclusion

The historical evolution of healthcare administration reflects broader changes in society, technology, and medical knowledge. From the early days of communal and religious care to the complex, technology-driven systems of today, healthcare administration has continually adapted to meet the needs of patients and communities.

Understanding this history helps us appreciate the complexities of modern healthcare administration and the continuous need for innovation and improvement. As we move forward, healthcare administrators will play a crucial role in navigating the challenges of an ever-evolving healthcare landscape, ensuring that healthcare systems are efficient, effective, and patient-centred.

CHAPTER 3: THE ROLE OF A HOSPITAL MANAGER

The role of a hospital manager is pivotal in ensuring the smooth operation of a healthcare facility. Hospital managers are responsible for overseeing the daily operations, managing staff, and ensuring that the hospital delivers high-quality patient care. This chapter delves into the various aspects of the role, highlighting the skills, responsibilities, and challenges that come with managing a hospital.

Key Responsibilities of a Hospital Manager

Hospital managers have a wide range of responsibilities that cover various aspects of hospital operations. These can be broadly categorised into leadership, operational management, financial management, human resources, quality and patient safety, and compliance.

Leadership and Strategic Planning

One of the primary roles of a hospital manager is to provide leadership and strategic direction. This involves setting the vision and mission of the hospital, developing long-term goals, and creating a roadmap to achieve them. Effective leadership requires the ability to inspire and motivate staff, foster a positive organisational culture, and ensure that all departments are aligned with the hospital's strategic objectives.

Strategic planning is a critical component of this role. Hospital managers must analyse market trends, assess the needs of the community, and develop strategies to address these needs. This includes identifying opportunities for growth, improving service delivery, and ensuring that the hospital remains competitive in the healthcare landscape.

Operational Management

Hospital managers are responsible for the day-to-day operations of the hospital. This includes managing patient admissions, coordinating with different departments, overseeing the maintenance of facilities, and ensuring that all services are delivered efficiently. Operational management requires a deep understanding of hospital workflows and the ability to identify and address any issues that may arise.

Effective operational management ensures that the hospital runs smoothly and that patients receive timely and appropriate care. Hospital managers must also ensure that the hospital is adequately staffed, that equipment and supplies are available, and that the physical environment is safe and conducive to patient care.

Financial Management

Managing the financial health of the hospital is another critical responsibility. Hospital managers must develop and oversee budgets, manage revenue and expenditures, and ensure that the hospital operates within its financial means. This involves monitoring financial performance, identifying cost-saving opportunities, and ensuring transparency in financial reporting.

Hospital managers must also secure funding for the hospital, which may involve negotiating contracts with insurance companies, seeking grants, and managing relationships with donors and other stakeholders. Effective financial management is essential for the sustainability of the hospital and the delivery of high-quality care.

Human Resources Management

The success of a hospital largely depends on its staff. Hospital managers are responsible for recruiting, training, and retaining skilled professionals. This includes managing employee relations, ensuring compliance with labour laws, and creating a positive work environment.

Human resources management also involves developing policies and procedures, managing performance evaluations, and addressing any staffing issues that may arise. Hospital managers must ensure that staff are adequately trained and supported, and that they have the resources they need to perform their jobs effectively.

Quality and Patient Safety

Ensuring the quality of care and patient safety is a top priority for hospital managers. This involves implementing quality assurance programs, monitoring clinical outcomes, and promoting a culture of continuous improvement. Hospital managers must ensure that the hospital complies with regulatory standards and best practices in patient care.

Patient safety initiatives may include infection control, medication safety, and patient safety education. Hospital managers must also ensure that adverse events are reported and addressed promptly, and that strategies are in place to prevent future occurrences.

Compliance and Legal Issues

Hospitals must comply with a myriad of regulations and laws. Hospital managers need to be well-versed in healthcare laws, accreditation standards, and ethical guidelines. They must ensure that the hospital operates within legal frameworks and maintains the highest ethical standards.

This includes ensuring compliance with health and safety regulations, managing risk, and overseeing the accreditation process. Hospital managers must also handle legal issues that may arise, such as patient complaints, malpractice claims, and employment disputes.

Skills and Qualities of an Effective Hospital Manager

Effective hospital managers possess a unique set of skills and qualities that enable them to navigate the complexities of healthcare management.

Leadership Skills

Strong leadership is essential for guiding teams, making strategic decisions, and fostering a positive organisational culture. Hospital managers must inspire confidence and lead by example, demonstrating a commitment to the hospital's mission and values.

Communication Skills

Effective communication is crucial for coordinating with staff, patients, and stakeholders. Hospital managers must be able to convey information clearly and listen actively to feedback and concerns. This includes managing conflicts, facilitating meetings, and ensuring that information flows smoothly across all levels of the organisation.

Analytical Skills

Hospital managers must analyse data to make informed decisions. This includes financial analysis, performance metrics, and patient outcomes. Being able to interpret complex information is vital for strategic planning and problem-solving.

Adaptability

The healthcare environment is dynamic, and hospital managers must be adaptable to change. This involves being open to new ideas, learning continuously, and responding effectively to unexpected challenges. Flexibility and resilience are key qualities that enable hospital managers to navigate the complexities of healthcare management.

Empathy and Compassion

Healthcare is inherently people-focused. Hospital managers must demonstrate empathy and compassion towards patients and staff, fostering an environment of care and respect. This involves understanding the needs and concerns of patients and staff and ensuring that these are addressed appropriately.

Problem-Solving Skills

Hospitals face a wide range of challenges, from operational issues to patient care concerns. Hospital managers must be adept at identifying problems, developing solutions, and implementing changes effectively. This requires critical thinking, creativity, and the ability to make decisions under pressure.

Challenges Faced by Hospital Managers

Managing a hospital comes with numerous challenges, many of which are unique to the healthcare sector.

Rising Costs

Healthcare costs are continually rising due to factors such as technological advancements, an ageing population, and increased demand for services. Hospital managers must find ways to control costs without compromising on the quality of care. This involves identifying cost-saving opportunities, negotiating contracts, and managing resources efficiently.

Regulatory Changes

Healthcare is a highly regulated industry, and hospitals must constantly adapt to new laws and regulations. This requires staying informed about changes and implementing necessary adjustments promptly. Hospital managers must ensure that the hospital remains compliant with all relevant regulations and that staff are aware of and adhere to these regulations.

Technological Advancements

The rapid pace of technological change in healthcare presents both opportunities and challenges. Hospital managers must assess new technologies, integrate them into existing systems, and ensure that staff are adequately trained. This includes managing the implementation of electronic health records (EHRs), telemedicine, and other health information technologies.

Patient Expectations

Patients today are more informed and have higher expectations regarding their care. Hospital managers must focus on improving patient satisfaction and experience, which involves enhancing communication, reducing wait times, and ensuring compassionate care. Meeting these expectations requires a patient-centred approach and a commitment to continuous improvement.

Workforce Management

Recruiting and retaining skilled healthcare professionals is a significant challenge. Hospital managers must address issues such as staff burnout, continuing education, and creating a positive work environment to maintain a competent and motivated workforce. This involves developing strategies for staff retention, providing opportunities for professional development, and ensuring that staff feel valued and supported.

Conclusion

The role of a hospital manager is multifaceted and challenging, requiring a unique blend of leadership, strategic planning, and operational expertise. Hospital managers play a critical role in ensuring that healthcare facilities operate efficiently, deliver high-quality care, and adapt to the ever-changing healthcare landscape. By understanding the key responsibilities, skills, and challenges associated with this role, current and aspiring hospital managers can better prepare themselves to lead healthcare facilities towards success.

In the next chapter, we will explore the importance of strategic planning in healthcare and provide a framework for developing effective strategies. This will include analysing market trends, assessing community needs, and identifying opportunities for growth and improvement.

CHAPTER 4: STRATEGIC PLANNING IN HEALTHCARE

Strategic planning is a critical component of effective healthcare management. It involves setting long-term goals, identifying the necessary resources, and developing a roadmap to achieve these objectives. For hospital managers, strategic planning is essential to ensure the hospital can adapt to changes in the healthcare environment, meet the needs of the community, and maintain financial stability. This chapter delves into the importance of strategic planning in healthcare, the steps involved in the process, and the tools and techniques used to develop and implement effective strategies.

The Importance of Strategic Planning in Healthcare

Strategic planning in healthcare serves several vital functions:

1. **Direction and Focus**: It provides a clear direction and focus for the organisation, ensuring that all efforts are aligned with the hospital's mission, vision, and goals.

2. **Resource Allocation**: It helps in the effective allocation of resources, ensuring that financial, human, and technological resources are used efficiently and effectively.

3. **Adaptability**: It prepares the hospital to adapt to changes in the healthcare environment, such as regulatory changes, technological advancements, and shifts in patient demographics.

4. **Performance Measurement**: It establishes benchmarks and performance indicators that can be used to measure progress and assess the effectiveness of strategies.

5. **Stakeholder Engagement**: It involves engaging with stakeholders, including staff, patients, and the community, to ensure that their needs and expectations are met.

Steps in the Strategic Planning Process

The strategic planning process typically involves several key steps:

1. **Environmental Scanning**
2. **Internal Assessment**
3. **Setting Objectives**
4. **Strategy Development**

5. **Implementation**
6. **Evaluation and Control**

1. Environmental Scanning

Environmental scanning involves analysing external factors that can impact the hospital. This includes understanding the broader healthcare landscape, identifying trends and changes, and assessing potential threats and opportunities. Key elements of environmental scanning include:

- **Political and Regulatory Environment**: Understanding changes in healthcare laws, regulations, and policies that could affect hospital operations.
- **Economic Factors**: Assessing economic conditions, such as funding levels, reimbursement rates, and financial stability of the healthcare system.
- **Social and Demographic Trends**: Analysing changes in population demographics, health behaviours, and patient expectations.
- **Technological Advancements**: Identifying new technologies that could improve patient care, enhance operational efficiency, or reduce costs.
- **Competitive Landscape**: Evaluating the strengths and weaknesses of other healthcare providers in the area.

2. Internal Assessment

An internal assessment involves evaluating the hospital's strengths and weaknesses. This includes analysing resources, capabilities, and performance in key areas such as:

- **Financial Health**: Reviewing financial statements, budget performance, and funding sources.
- **Human Resources**: Assessing staffing levels, employee skills, and workforce satisfaction.
- **Operational Efficiency**: Evaluating processes, workflows, and utilisation of resources.

- **Quality of Care**: Analysing clinical outcomes, patient satisfaction, and adherence to best practices.
- **Organisational Culture**: Understanding the hospital's culture, values, and internal communication.

3. Setting Objectives

Setting clear and achievable objectives is a crucial step in the strategic planning process. Objectives should be:

- **Specific**: Clearly defined and unambiguous.
- **Measurable**: Quantifiable and able to be tracked over time.
- **Achievable**: Realistic and attainable given the hospital's resources and capabilities.
- **Relevant**: Aligned with the hospital's mission and strategic priorities.
- **Time-bound**: Set within a specific timeframe for completion.

4. Strategy Development

Once objectives are set, the next step is to develop strategies to achieve them. This involves identifying the actions needed to reach the objectives, allocating resources, and establishing timelines. Key considerations in strategy development include:

- **Resource Allocation**: Determining the necessary financial, human, and technological resources.
- **Risk Management**: Identifying potential risks and developing mitigation plans.
- **Stakeholder Engagement**: Involving key stakeholders in the planning process to ensure buy-in and support.
- **Contingency Planning**: Preparing for unexpected challenges or changes in the environment.

5. Implementation

Implementing the strategic plan involves putting the developed strategies into action. This requires effective project management, clear communication, and ongoing monitoring. Key steps in implementation include:

- **Assigning Responsibilities**: Designating individuals or teams to lead and oversee each strategy.
- **Establishing Timelines**: Setting specific deadlines for key milestones and deliverables.
- **Resource Deployment**: Allocating the necessary resources to support implementation.
- **Communication**: Ensuring that all stakeholders are informed about the plan and their roles.

6. Evaluation and Control

Evaluation and control involve monitoring progress, assessing performance, and making necessary adjustments to the plan. This ensures that the hospital stays on track to achieve its objectives. Key activities include:

- **Performance Measurement**: Using key performance indicators (KPIs) to track progress and outcomes.
- **Regular Reviews**: Conducting regular reviews of the strategic plan to assess performance and identify areas for improvement.
- **Feedback Mechanisms**: Gathering feedback from stakeholders to inform adjustments and refinements.
- **Continuous Improvement**: Implementing changes and improvements based on evaluation findings.

Tools and Techniques for Strategic Planning

Several tools and techniques can assist hospital managers in the strategic planning process:

1. **SWOT Analysis**: SWOT (Strengths, Weaknesses, Opportunities, Threats) analysis helps in identifying internal

strengths and weaknesses, as well as external opportunities and threats. It provides a comprehensive overview of the hospital's current position and potential future challenges and opportunities.

2. **PEST Analysis**: PEST (Political, Economic, Social, Technological) analysis focuses on external factors that can impact the hospital. It helps in understanding the broader environment and identifying trends and changes that could affect the hospital's strategic direction.

3. **Balanced Scorecard**: The balanced scorecard is a performance management tool that helps in translating the hospital's vision and strategy into specific, measurable objectives. It considers multiple perspectives, including financial performance, patient satisfaction, internal processes, and learning and growth.

4. **Scenario Planning**: Scenario planning involves developing different scenarios based on potential future events and assessing their impact on the hospital. It helps in preparing for uncertainties and developing flexible strategies.

5. **Benchmarking**: Benchmarking involves comparing the hospital's performance with that of other similar institutions. It helps in identifying best practices, setting performance standards, and identifying areas for improvement.

Conclusion

Strategic planning is a critical function for hospital managers, enabling them to navigate the complexities of the healthcare environment and ensure the long-term success of their organisations. By systematically assessing the external environment, evaluating internal capabilities, setting clear objectives, and developing actionable strategies, hospital managers can position their hospitals for growth and improvement. The tools and techniques discussed in this chapter provide a framework for effective strategic planning, helping hospital managers to make informed decisions and achieve their strategic goals.

In the next chapter, we will explore financial management in healthcare, focusing on budgeting, financial analysis, and strategies for maintaining financial stability. This will include practical insights into managing hospital finances and ensuring the efficient use of resources to support the delivery of high-quality care.

CHAPTER 5: FINANCIAL MANAGEMENT IN HOSPITALS

Financial management is a cornerstone of hospital administration, crucial for ensuring that healthcare facilities can operate efficiently, provide high-quality care, and remain financially sustainable. Effective financial management involves budgeting, financial analysis, cost control, and revenue generation. This chapter explores the key aspects of financial management in hospitals, offering insights into best practices and strategies for maintaining financial health.

The Importance of Financial Management in Hospitals

Financial management in hospitals is vital for several reasons:

1. **Sustainability**: Ensuring the long-term financial health of the hospital allows it to continue providing essential services to the community.

2. **Resource Allocation**: Efficient financial management enables the optimal allocation of resources, ensuring that funds are available where they are most needed.
3. **Quality of Care**: Adequate financial resources are necessary to maintain and improve the quality of patient care.
4. **Compliance**: Hospitals must comply with financial regulations and reporting requirements, necessitating robust financial management systems.
5. **Risk Management**: Identifying and mitigating financial risks helps protect the hospital from unexpected financial difficulties.

Key Components of Financial Management

Effective financial management in hospitals involves several key components, each of which plays a critical role in ensuring financial stability and operational efficiency.

Budgeting

Budgeting is the process of creating a plan to allocate the hospital's financial resources. It involves projecting revenue, estimating expenses, and determining how funds will be distributed across different departments and services. Key steps in the budgeting process include:

1. **Revenue Forecasting**: Estimating the hospital's income from various sources, such as patient services, insurance reimbursements, government funding, and donations.
2. **Expense Estimation**: Predicting the costs associated with operating the hospital, including salaries, medical supplies, utilities, maintenance, and administrative expenses.
3. **Budget Preparation**: Developing a detailed budget that outlines expected revenues and expenditures, and aligning them with the hospital's strategic goals.
4. **Monitoring and Adjusting**: Regularly reviewing budget performance and making necessary adjustments to address variances and ensure financial targets are met.

Financial Analysis

Financial analysis involves evaluating the hospital's financial performance using various metrics and tools. This process helps hospital managers make informed decisions, identify areas for improvement, and ensure financial sustainability. Key elements of financial analysis include:

1. **Financial Statements**: Reviewing income statements, balance sheets, and cash flow statements to assess the hospital's financial health.
2. **Ratio Analysis**: Using financial ratios, such as profitability ratios, liquidity ratios, and efficiency ratios, to evaluate the hospital's performance and compare it with industry benchmarks.
3. **Trend Analysis**: Analysing financial data over time to identify trends and patterns that can inform decision-making.
4. **Variance Analysis**: Comparing actual financial performance with budgeted figures to identify and address deviations.

Cost Control

Cost control is essential for managing expenses and ensuring the efficient use of resources. Hospital managers must implement strategies to control costs without compromising the quality of care. Key cost control strategies include:

1. **Expense Monitoring**: Regularly reviewing and analysing expenses to identify areas of overspending and opportunities for cost savings.
2. **Efficiency Improvements**: Streamlining processes and workflows to reduce waste and improve operational efficiency.
3. **Negotiating Contracts**: Securing favourable terms with suppliers, vendors, and service providers to minimise costs.

4. **Utilisation Management**: Ensuring that medical services and resources are used appropriately and efficiently to avoid unnecessary costs.

Revenue Generation

Revenue generation is a critical aspect of financial management, ensuring that the hospital has sufficient funds to operate and invest in improvements. Key strategies for revenue generation include:

1. **Billing and Collections**: Implementing efficient billing and collections processes to ensure timely and accurate payment for services rendered.
2. **Insurance Reimbursements**: Maximising reimbursements from insurance companies by ensuring accurate coding and documentation of services.
3. **Diversifying Revenue Streams**: Exploring additional revenue sources, such as offering specialised services, participating in research projects, or establishing partnerships with other healthcare providers.
4. **Fundraising and Grants**: Securing donations, grants, and other forms of external funding to support hospital operations and initiatives.

Best Practices in Financial Management

Adopting best practices in financial management can help hospital managers maintain financial stability and achieve their strategic goals. Some key best practices include:

Developing a Comprehensive Financial Plan

A comprehensive financial plan outlines the hospital's financial goals, strategies, and action plans. It provides a roadmap for achieving financial sustainability and supports informed decision-making. The financial plan should include:

1. **Revenue Projections**: Detailed forecasts of expected income from various sources.
2. **Expense Projections**: Estimates of operational and capital expenditures.
3. **Capital Planning**: Plans for major investments, such as facility upgrades, new equipment, and technology improvements.
4. **Contingency Plans**: Strategies for addressing potential financial challenges and risks.

Implementing Robust Financial Controls

Robust financial controls help ensure the accuracy and integrity of financial transactions and reporting. Key controls include:

1. **Internal Audits**: Regular internal audits to review financial processes, identify weaknesses, and ensure compliance with policies and regulations.
2. **Segregation of Duties**: Dividing financial responsibilities among different staff members to prevent fraud and errors.
3. **Approval Processes**: Implementing approval processes for significant financial transactions to ensure oversight and accountability.
4. **Financial Reporting**: Regularly generating and reviewing financial reports to monitor performance and inform decision-making.

Enhancing Financial Transparency

Transparency in financial management builds trust with stakeholders and supports accountability. Hospitals should:

1. **Communicate Financial Performance**: Regularly communicate financial performance to staff, board members, and other stakeholders.

2. **Engage Stakeholders**: Involve stakeholders in financial planning and decision-making processes to ensure their perspectives and needs are considered.
3. **Provide Training**: Offer training and resources to staff to enhance their understanding of financial management and reporting.

Leveraging Technology

Technology can significantly enhance financial management processes, improving efficiency and accuracy. Key technologies include:

1. **Financial Management Systems**: Implementing integrated financial management systems to streamline budgeting, accounting, and reporting processes.
2. **Data Analytics**: Using data analytics tools to analyse financial data, identify trends, and support decision-making.
3. **Electronic Health Records (EHRs)**: Integrating EHRs with financial systems to improve billing accuracy and efficiency.

Challenges in Financial Management

Hospital managers face several challenges in financial management, including:

Rising Healthcare Costs

The cost of healthcare continues to rise due to factors such as technological advancements, an ageing population, and increasing demand for services. Hospital managers must find ways to control costs while maintaining the quality of care.

Regulatory Changes

Changes in healthcare regulations and reimbursement policies can impact hospital finances. Managers must stay informed about regulatory changes and adapt their financial strategies accordingly.

Revenue Cycle Management

Effective revenue cycle management is crucial for ensuring timely and accurate payment for services. Hospital managers must address challenges such as billing errors, insurance denials, and patient payment issues.

Financial Sustainability

Maintaining financial sustainability requires balancing short-term financial pressures with long-term strategic goals. Hospital managers must make strategic investments while ensuring that day-to-day operations remain financially viable.

Conclusion

Financial management is a critical function for hospital managers, encompassing budgeting, financial analysis, cost control, and revenue generation. Effective financial management ensures that hospitals can operate efficiently, provide high-quality care, and remain financially sustainable. By adopting best practices and leveraging technology, hospital managers can navigate financial challenges and achieve their strategic goals.

In the next chapter, we will explore the importance of quality and patient safety in healthcare. We will discuss strategies for implementing quality assurance programs, monitoring clinical outcomes, and fostering a culture of continuous improvement. This will include practical insights into ensuring patient safety and delivering high-quality care.

CHAPTER 6: HUMAN RESOURCES MANAGEMENT

Human resources management (HRM) is an essential function in any organisation, and it is particularly critical in healthcare settings. Effective HRM ensures that hospitals have the right number of skilled staff, working in a supportive environment, to deliver high-quality patient care. This chapter explores the key aspects of HRM in hospitals, including recruitment, training, retention, performance management, and the importance of a positive organisational culture.

The Importance of Human Resources Management in Hospitals

HRM is vital in hospitals for several reasons:

1. **Staffing**: Ensuring the hospital has sufficient, qualified staff to meet patient care demands.
2. **Employee Satisfaction**: Creating a work environment that promotes job satisfaction and reduces turnover.
3. **Compliance**: Adhering to labour laws, healthcare regulations, and accreditation standards.
4. **Quality of Care**: Supporting staff in delivering high-quality patient care through adequate training and resources.
5. **Organisational Culture**: Fostering a culture of collaboration, respect, and continuous improvement.

Key Components of Human Resources Management

Effective HRM in hospitals involves several key components, each critical for maintaining a motivated, competent, and satisfied workforce.

Recruitment and Selection

Recruiting the right people is the foundation of effective HRM. Hospitals must attract, select, and retain individuals who are not only qualified but also aligned with the hospital's values and culture. Key steps in the recruitment and selection process include:

1. **Job Analysis and Descriptions**: Clearly defining the roles and responsibilities for each position to attract suitable candidates.
2. **Sourcing Candidates**: Using various channels such as job boards, recruitment agencies, and professional networks to find potential employees.
3. **Screening and Interviewing**: Assessing candidates through interviews, tests, and background checks to ensure they meet the required qualifications and fit with the hospital's culture.
4. **Onboarding**: Providing new hires with a comprehensive orientation to help them integrate into the hospital and understand their roles.

Training and Development

Ongoing training and development are crucial for ensuring that hospital staff maintain their skills and stay updated with the latest medical advancements and best practices. Key elements include:

1. **Induction Training**: Introducing new employees to the hospital's policies, procedures, and culture.
2. **Continuous Professional Development (CPD)**: Offering regular training sessions, workshops, and courses to help staff develop their skills and knowledge.
3. **Leadership Development**: Providing training for current and potential leaders to ensure effective management and succession planning.
4. **Compliance Training**: Ensuring staff are aware of and comply with relevant laws and regulations, including health and safety, patient confidentiality, and ethical standards.

Retention Strategies

Retaining skilled and experienced staff is essential for maintaining high-quality patient care and operational stability. Effective retention strategies include:

1. **Competitive Compensation**: Offering competitive salaries and benefits to attract and retain top talent.
2. **Career Development**: Providing opportunities for career advancement and professional growth.
3. **Work-Life Balance**: Promoting work-life balance through flexible working hours, job sharing, and supportive policies.
4. **Recognition and Rewards**: Recognising and rewarding employees' achievements and contributions to the hospital.

Performance Management

Performance management involves evaluating and improving employee performance to ensure that hospital staff meet their objectives and contribute to the hospital's goals. Key components include:

1. **Goal Setting**: Setting clear, achievable goals for employees and aligning them with the hospital's strategic objectives.
2. **Performance Reviews**: Conducting regular performance appraisals to assess employee performance, provide feedback, and identify areas for improvement.
3. **Professional Development Plans**: Creating individual development plans to help employees improve their skills and advance their careers.
4. **Managing Underperformance**: Addressing performance issues through coaching, additional training, or, if necessary, disciplinary action.

Organisational Culture

A positive organisational culture is critical for employee satisfaction, retention, and overall hospital performance. Key elements of fostering a positive culture include:

1. **Leadership**: Effective leadership that promotes a clear vision, mission, and values.
2. **Communication**: Open, transparent, and consistent communication between management and staff.
3. **Collaboration**: Encouraging teamwork and collaboration across different departments and roles.
4. **Respect and Inclusivity**: Promoting a culture of respect, inclusivity, and diversity.

Best Practices in Human Resources Management

Adopting best practices in HRM can help hospital managers create a supportive and efficient work environment. Some key best practices include:

Developing Comprehensive HR Policies

Comprehensive HR policies provide a framework for managing staff and ensuring consistency in HR practices. Key policies include:

1. **Recruitment and Selection**: Clear guidelines for attracting and selecting candidates.
2. **Equal Opportunity and Diversity**: Policies that promote diversity and prevent discrimination.
3. **Employee Conduct**: Standards for professional behaviour and conduct.
4. **Health and Safety**: Ensuring a safe working environment for all staff.

Implementing Effective Communication Channels

Effective communication is essential for ensuring that staff are informed, engaged, and able to provide feedback. Key communication strategies include:

1. **Regular Meetings**: Holding regular staff meetings to discuss updates, issues, and feedback.
2. **Feedback Systems**: Implementing systems for employees to provide feedback and suggestions.
3. **Internal Communications**: Using newsletters, intranets, and bulletin boards to share important information.

Promoting Employee Wellbeing

Supporting employee wellbeing is crucial for maintaining a motivated and productive workforce. Key strategies include:

1. **Wellbeing Programs**: Offering programs and resources to support physical, mental, and emotional wellbeing.
2. **Support Services**: Providing access to counselling, support groups, and employee assistance programs.
3. **Healthy Work Environment**: Ensuring a safe, healthy, and supportive work environment.

Leveraging Technology

Technology can enhance HRM processes, making them more efficient and effective. Key technologies include:

1. **HR Management Systems (HRMS)**: Implementing HRMS to streamline recruitment, onboarding, performance management, and employee records.
2. **E-Learning Platforms**: Using e-learning platforms to provide accessible and flexible training options.
3. **Employee Self-Service**: Implementing self-service portals for employees to access HR services and information.

Challenges in Human Resources Management

Hospital managers face several challenges in HRM, including:

Workforce Shortages

Shortages of skilled healthcare professionals can impact patient care and increase staff workload. Managers must develop strategies to attract and retain talent and ensure that staffing levels are sufficient to meet demand.

Staff Burnout

Healthcare workers often face high levels of stress and burnout, which can affect their performance and wellbeing. Managers must address the causes of burnout and provide support to staff.

Compliance with Regulations

Hospitals must comply with numerous labour laws and healthcare regulations. Managers need to stay informed about changes in legislation and ensure that the hospital's HR policies and practices are compliant.

Managing Diversity

Hospitals employ a diverse workforce, and managers must create an inclusive environment that respects and values differences. This involves providing diversity training, addressing bias, and promoting inclusivity.

Conclusion

Human resources management is a critical function for hospital managers, encompassing recruitment, training, retention, performance management, and organisational culture. Effective HRM ensures that hospitals have the skilled, motivated, and satisfied staff needed to deliver high-quality patient care. By adopting best practices and addressing HRM challenges, hospital managers can create a supportive and efficient work environment that promotes employee satisfaction and operational success.

In the next chapter, we will explore quality and patient safety in healthcare. We will discuss strategies for implementing quality assurance programs, monitoring clinical outcomes, and fostering a culture of continuous improvement. This will include practical insights into ensuring patient safety and delivering high-quality care.

CHAPTER 7: QUALITY AND PATIENT SAFETY

Quality and patient safety are paramount in healthcare management. Ensuring high standards of care while minimising risks and errors is a fundamental responsibility of hospital managers. This chapter delves into the principles of quality and patient safety, the strategies for implementing effective quality assurance programs, and the importance of fostering a culture of continuous improvement.

The Importance of Quality and Patient Safety

Quality and patient safety in healthcare are critical for several reasons:

1. **Patient Outcomes**: Ensuring high-quality care directly impacts patient health and recovery.
2. **Reputation**: High standards of care enhance the hospital's reputation and patient trust.
3. **Regulatory Compliance**: Compliance with healthcare regulations and standards is mandatory and directly linked to quality and safety.

4. **Cost Efficiency**: Reducing errors and improving processes can lower costs associated with corrective actions, legal issues, and longer patient stays.
5. **Employee Satisfaction**: A focus on quality and safety creates a better work environment, leading to higher staff morale and retention.

Key Components of Quality and Patient Safety

To effectively manage quality and patient safety, hospitals must focus on several key components:

Quality Assurance Programs

Quality assurance (QA) programs are designed to systematically monitor and evaluate the quality of care provided in a hospital. Key elements of QA programs include:

1. **Standards and Guidelines**: Establishing clear standards and clinical guidelines to ensure consistent, high-quality care.
2. **Performance Indicators**: Defining key performance indicators (KPIs) to measure and track quality outcomes.
3. **Audits and Reviews**: Conducting regular audits and reviews of clinical practices, patient outcomes, and operational processes.
4. **Continuous Improvement**: Implementing a continuous improvement process to address identified issues and enhance care quality.

Risk Management

Risk management involves identifying, assessing, and mitigating risks to patient safety. Key steps in risk management include:

1. **Risk Identification**: Identifying potential risks through incident reporting, audits, and feedback from staff and patients.

2. **Risk Assessment**: Evaluating the likelihood and impact of identified risks.
3. **Risk Mitigation**: Developing and implementing strategies to mitigate risks, such as staff training, process changes, and safety protocols.
4. **Incident Reporting**: Establishing a system for reporting and analysing incidents to prevent future occurrences.

Patient Safety Culture

Fostering a culture of safety within the hospital is essential for ensuring that patient safety is a shared responsibility. Key elements include:

1. **Leadership Commitment**: Leaders must demonstrate a commitment to patient safety through their actions and decisions.
2. **Open Communication**: Encouraging open communication and transparency about safety issues and incidents.
3. **Staff Empowerment**: Empowering staff to speak up about safety concerns and participate in safety initiatives.
4. **Learning Environment**: Creating an environment where staff can learn from errors and near misses without fear of punishment.

Strategies for Ensuring Quality and Patient Safety

Several strategies can help hospital managers ensure quality and patient safety:

Implementing Clinical Pathways

Clinical pathways are structured multidisciplinary care plans that outline the essential steps in the care of patients with specific clinical problems. Benefits include:

1. **Standardisation**: Ensuring consistent care based on best practices.
2. **Efficiency**: Streamlining processes and reducing unnecessary variations in care.
3. **Improved Outcomes**: Enhancing patient outcomes through evidence-based practices.

Adopting Evidence-Based Practices

Evidence-based practices involve using the best available research evidence to guide clinical decision-making. Key steps include:

1. **Research and Guidelines**: Staying updated with the latest research and clinical guidelines.
2. **Training and Education**: Providing ongoing training for staff on evidence-based practices.
3. **Implementation**: Integrating evidence-based practices into clinical protocols and pathways.

Utilising Health Information Technology

Health information technology (HIT) can significantly enhance quality and patient safety. Key technologies include:

1. **Electronic Health Records (EHRs)**: Improving accuracy and accessibility of patient information.
2. **Clinical Decision Support Systems (CDSS)**: Providing real-time support to clinicians in making informed decisions.
3. **Telemedicine**: Expanding access to care and enabling remote monitoring and consultations.

Engaging Patients and Families

Engaging patients and their families in the care process is crucial for ensuring quality and safety. Key strategies include:

1. **Education**: Providing patients and families with information about their condition and treatment options.
2. **Involvement**: Involving patients and families in care decisions and planning.
3. **Feedback**: Collecting feedback from patients and families to identify areas for improvement.

Monitoring and Evaluating Quality and Patient Safety

Continuous monitoring and evaluation are essential for maintaining and improving quality and patient safety. Key activities include:

Data Collection and Analysis

Collecting and analysing data on various aspects of care can help identify trends, measure performance, and pinpoint areas for improvement. Key steps include:

1. **Data Sources**: Using a variety of data sources, such as patient records, surveys, and incident reports.
2. **Analytics**: Applying statistical and analytical tools to interpret data and identify patterns.
3. **Reporting**: Creating regular reports to communicate findings to staff and stakeholders.

Performance Measurement

Measuring performance against established benchmarks and standards is critical for assessing quality and safety. Key performance indicators (KPIs) might include:

1. **Clinical Outcomes**: Metrics such as infection rates, readmission rates, and mortality rates.
2. **Patient Satisfaction**: Surveys and feedback measuring patient experiences and satisfaction.
3. **Process Efficiency**: Metrics related to operational efficiency, such as average length of stay and wait times.

Quality Improvement Initiatives

Quality improvement (QI) initiatives involve using the data and insights gained from monitoring and evaluation to drive improvements. Key components include:

1. **Plan-Do-Study-Act (PDSA) Cycles**: A structured approach to testing and implementing changes.
2. **Root Cause Analysis**: Identifying the underlying causes of problems to develop effective solutions.
3. **Multidisciplinary Teams**: Engaging teams from various disciplines to collaboratively address quality and safety issues.

Challenges in Quality and Patient Safety

Hospital managers face several challenges in ensuring quality and patient safety, including:

Resource Constraints

Limited financial and human resources can impact the ability to implement and sustain quality and safety initiatives. Managers must prioritise resources effectively and seek external funding or partnerships when necessary.

Resistance to Change

Resistance to change from staff can hinder the adoption of new practices and technologies. Managers must engage and involve staff in the change process, providing training and support to facilitate transitions.

Regulatory Compliance

Keeping up with changing regulations and standards can be challenging. Managers must stay informed and ensure that the hospital's policies and practices comply with current requirements.

Conclusion

Quality and patient safety are fundamental to hospital management, directly impacting patient outcomes, staff satisfaction, and the hospital's reputation. By implementing effective quality assurance programs, fostering a culture of safety, and continuously monitoring and improving performance, hospital managers can ensure that their hospitals deliver high-quality, safe care.

In the next chapter, we will explore the role of technology in healthcare. We will discuss the impact of digital transformation on hospital operations, the benefits and challenges of health information technology, and the future trends in healthcare innovation. This will include practical insights into leveraging technology to enhance patient care and operational efficiency.

CHAPTER 8: INFORMATION TECHNOLOGY IN HEALTHCARE

Information Technology (IT) has revolutionised healthcare, transforming how patient care is delivered, managed, and improved. The integration of IT in healthcare has led to enhanced efficiency, improved patient outcomes, and more robust data management systems. This chapter explores the role of IT in healthcare, the benefits and challenges of health information technology, and future trends in healthcare innovation.

The Role of Information Technology in Healthcare

Information technology plays a crucial role in modern healthcare systems, supporting a wide range of activities and functions. Key areas where IT impacts healthcare include:

1. **Electronic Health Records (EHRs)**: Digital versions of patients' paper charts, providing real-time, patient-centred records that make information available instantly and securely to authorised users.
2. **Telemedicine**: The use of telecommunication technology to provide clinical health care at a distance, expanding access to medical services.
3. **Health Information Exchange (HIE)**: The electronic sharing of health-related information among medical facilities, ensuring that patient data is available wherever and whenever it is needed.
4. **Clinical Decision Support Systems (CDSS)**: Computer systems designed to assist healthcare providers in making clinical decisions, improving diagnostic accuracy and treatment efficacy.
5. **Patient Portals**: Secure online platforms that provide patients with access to their health information and enable communication with healthcare providers.

Benefits of Health Information Technology

The adoption of health information technology offers numerous benefits, including:

Improved Patient Care

1. **Accuracy and Efficiency**: EHRs reduce errors associated with manual record-keeping and ensure that patient information is accurate, complete, and up-to-date.
2. **Better Coordination**: Health information exchange facilitates better coordination of care among different healthcare providers, leading to more cohesive and efficient patient care.
3. **Enhanced Diagnostics**: CDSS provide evidence-based recommendations and alerts, helping clinicians make more informed decisions and reducing the likelihood of diagnostic errors.

Increased Accessibility

1. **Telemedicine**: Telemedicine expands access to care, especially for patients in remote or underserved areas, by enabling consultations and follow-ups via video conferencing.
2. **Patient Portals**: Patient portals empower patients by giving them access to their health records, test results, and the ability to schedule appointments and communicate with their healthcare providers.

Operational Efficiency

1. **Streamlined Processes**: Automated systems reduce administrative burdens, streamline workflows, and improve overall efficiency in healthcare settings.
2. **Cost Savings**: By reducing errors, improving efficiency, and minimising redundant tests and procedures, health IT can lead to significant cost savings for healthcare organisations.

Enhanced Data Management

1. **Data Analytics**: Advanced data analytics tools can analyse large volumes of health data to identify trends, predict outcomes, and support research and public health initiatives.

2. **Security and Compliance**: Health IT systems enhance data security and help ensure compliance with regulations such as the General Data Protection Regulation (GDPR) and the Health Insurance Portability and Accountability Act (HIPAA).

Challenges of Health Information Technology

Despite the benefits, the implementation and use of health IT also present several challenges:

High Implementation Costs

1. **Initial Investment**: The cost of purchasing, implementing, and maintaining health IT systems can be significant, posing a barrier for some healthcare organisations.
2. **Training and Support**: Ongoing training and support are necessary to ensure that staff can effectively use new technologies, adding to the overall costs.

Data Privacy and Security

1. **Cybersecurity Threats**: Healthcare data is a prime target for cyberattacks, requiring robust security measures to protect sensitive patient information.
2. **Compliance**: Ensuring compliance with various data protection regulations can be complex and resource-intensive.

Interoperability

Interoperability refers to the ability of different information technology systems and software applications to communicate, exchange data, and use the information that has been exchanged. In the context of healthcare, interoperability specifically refers to the capability of various healthcare information systems and software applications to securely exchange patient information across different healthcare providers, organisations, and geographic regions. This exchange of data allows for seamless and coordinated care delivery, improves patient outcomes, and enhances overall healthcare efficiency. Interoperability ensures that health information can be accessed, shared, and used reliably by authorised individuals and systems when and where it is needed to support patient care.

1. **System Integration**: Integrating different health IT systems to ensure seamless data exchange can be challenging due to varying standards and protocols.
2. **Data Silos**: Fragmented data systems can create silos, hindering the efficient sharing and use of health information.

User Resistance

1. **Change Management**: Resistance to change among healthcare providers and staff can impede the adoption of new technologies.
2. **Usability Issues**: Poorly designed systems can lead to frustration and decreased productivity among users.

Future Trends in Healthcare IT

The future of healthcare IT is shaped by several emerging trends and innovations:

Artificial Intelligence (AI) and Machine Learning (ML)

1. **Predictive Analytics**: AI and ML algorithms can analyse vast amounts of data to predict patient outcomes, identify at-risk populations, and support preventive care.
2. **Automated Diagnostics**: AI-powered tools can assist in diagnosing conditions by analysing medical images, lab results, and patient records, improving accuracy and efficiency.

Blockchain Technology

1. **Data Security**: Blockchain technology offers enhanced security for health data by creating immutable and decentralised records.

2. **Interoperability**: Blockchain can facilitate secure and transparent data sharing among different healthcare entities, improving interoperability.

Internet of Medical Things (IoMT)

1. **Wearable Devices**: Wearable health devices can monitor vital signs, activity levels, and other health metrics in real time, providing valuable data for both patients and healthcare providers.
2. **Remote Monitoring**: IoMT enables remote monitoring of patients with chronic conditions, reducing hospital visits and improving patient management.

Personalised Medicine

1. **Genomics and Big Data**: Advances in genomics and the analysis of large datasets enable personalised treatment plans based on an individual's genetic makeup and health history.
2. **Tailored Treatments**: Personalised medicine offers the potential for more effective and targeted treatments, improving patient outcomes.

Implementing Health IT: Best Practices

To successfully implement and leverage health IT, hospital managers should consider the following best practices:

Comprehensive Planning

1. **Needs Assessment**: Conduct a thorough assessment of the hospital's needs and objectives to determine the most suitable IT solutions.
2. **Strategic Planning**: Develop a clear strategic plan that outlines the goals, timelines, and resources required for implementation.

Stakeholder Engagement

1. **Involving Staff**: Engage healthcare providers, staff, and patients in the planning and implementation process to ensure their needs and concerns are addressed.
2. **Communication**: Maintain open lines of communication to keep all stakeholders informed and involved throughout the process.

Training and Support

1. **Comprehensive Training**: Provide comprehensive training programs to ensure that all users are proficient in using the new systems.
2. **Ongoing Support**: Establish ongoing support mechanisms, such as help desks and user groups, to address any issues and provide assistance as needed.

Monitoring and Evaluation

1. **Performance Metrics**: Define and monitor key performance metrics to assess the effectiveness of the IT systems and identify areas for improvement.
2. **Feedback Loops**: Implement feedback loops to gather input from users and make necessary adjustments to optimise the systems.

Conclusion

Information technology has the potential to transform healthcare, improving patient care, operational efficiency, and data management. By embracing the benefits and addressing the challenges of health IT, hospital managers can enhance the quality and safety of care, streamline operations, and drive innovation. As technology continues to evolve, staying abreast of emerging trends and best practices will be essential for maximising the potential of health IT in healthcare.

In the next chapter, we will explore healthcare marketing and public relations. We will discuss strategies for effectively communicating with patients and the community, building the hospital's brand, and managing public perception. This will include practical insights into leveraging digital marketing, social media, and community engagement to enhance the hospital's reputation and reach.

CHAPTER 9: LEGAL AND ETHICAL CONSIDERATIONS

Legal and ethical considerations are paramount in healthcare management, guiding the conduct of healthcare professionals, ensuring patient rights, and maintaining public trust. This chapter explores the fundamental legal and ethical principles in healthcare, the responsibilities of hospital managers in upholding these standards, and the challenges they may face.

Legal Considerations in Healthcare

Healthcare is governed by a complex framework of laws and regulations designed to protect patient rights, ensure the quality of care, and maintain ethical standards. Key legal considerations include:

Patient Rights and Confidentiality

1. **Informed Consent**: Patients have the right to receive detailed information about their medical condition, treatment options, potential risks, and benefits before consenting to treatment.
2. **Confidentiality**: Healthcare providers are legally obligated to protect patient confidentiality, ensuring that personal and medical information is kept private and shared only with authorised individuals.
3. **Right to Treatment**: Patients have the right to access necessary medical treatment without discrimination.

Regulatory Compliance

1. **Licensing and Accreditation**: Hospitals must comply with national and state regulations regarding licensing, accreditation, and certification to ensure they meet required standards of care.
2. **Health and Safety Regulations**: Compliance with health and safety regulations is crucial to protect patients, staff, and visitors from harm.
3. **Data Protection Laws**: Hospitals must adhere to data protection laws such as the General Data Protection Regulation (GDPR) to safeguard patient information.

Medical Malpractice and Liability

1. **Duty of Care**: Healthcare providers have a legal duty to provide a standard of care that is reasonable and consistent with the medical profession's accepted practices.
2. **Negligence**: Failure to meet the standard of care can result in legal liability for negligence if it causes harm to the patient.
3. **Litigation and Compensation**: Hospitals must have processes in place to manage litigation and provide

compensation to patients harmed by medical errors or negligence.

Ethical Considerations in Healthcare

Ethical principles guide healthcare providers in making decisions that respect patient autonomy, beneficence, non-maleficence, and justice. Key ethical considerations include:

Autonomy

1. **Respect for Patient Autonomy**: Healthcare providers must respect patients' rights to make informed decisions about their care, including the right to refuse treatment.
2. **Advance Directives**: Patients have the right to make advance directives regarding their healthcare preferences in case they become unable to make decisions in the future.

Beneficence and non-maleficence

1. **Beneficence**: Healthcare providers must act in the best interest of the patient, promoting well-being and providing beneficial care.
2. **Non-Maleficence**: The principle of "do no harm" requires healthcare providers to avoid causing harm to patients through their actions or omissions.

Justice

1. **Equity in Healthcare**: Healthcare providers must ensure that care is provided fairly and equitably, without discrimination based on race, gender, socioeconomic status, or other factors.
2. **Resource Allocation**: Ethical considerations must guide the allocation of limited healthcare resources, ensuring that decisions are made fairly and transparently.

The Role of Hospital Managers in Legal and Ethical Compliance

Hospital managers play a critical role in ensuring that their institutions adhere to legal and ethical standards. Their responsibilities include:

Policy Development and Implementation

1. **Developing Policies**: Creating and implementing policies that reflect legal requirements and ethical principles, covering areas such as patient rights, confidentiality, informed consent, and non-discrimination.
2. **Training and Education**: Providing regular training and education for staff on legal and ethical issues, ensuring they understand and adhere to relevant standards and practices.

Monitoring and Compliance

1. **Compliance Programmes**: Establishing compliance programmes to monitor adherence to legal and ethical standards, including regular audits, risk assessments, and reporting mechanisms.
2. **Incident Reporting**: Implementing systems for reporting and investigating incidents, ensuring that any breaches of legal or ethical standards are addressed promptly and appropriately.

Ethical Decision-Making

1. **Ethics Committees**: Forming ethics committees to provide guidance on complex ethical issues, support decision-making, and resolve ethical dilemmas.
2. **Stakeholder Engagement**: Engaging with patients, families, staff, and the community to ensure that ethical considerations are integrated into healthcare delivery and decision-making processes.

Challenges in Legal and Ethical Compliance

Hospital managers may face several challenges in ensuring legal and ethical compliance, including:

Conflicts of Interest

1. **Balancing Interests**: Managers must navigate conflicts of interest, balancing the needs and rights of patients, staff, and the institution.
2. **Transparency**: Ensuring transparency and accountability in decision-making processes to maintain trust and integrity.

Resource Constraints

1. **Limited Resources**: Resource constraints can make it difficult to provide equitable care and meet all legal and ethical standards.
2. **Prioritisation**: Managers must prioritise resource allocation in a way that aligns with ethical principles and legal obligations.

Rapid Technological Advances

1. **New Ethical Issues**: Advances in medical technology can create new ethical issues and dilemmas, such as those related to genetic testing, artificial intelligence, and end-of-life care.
2. **Regulatory Lag**: Legal frameworks may lag behind technological advancements, creating uncertainty and challenges for compliance.

Conclusion

Legal and ethical considerations are fundamental to healthcare management, ensuring that patient rights are protected, care is delivered safely and equitably, and public trust is maintained.

Hospital managers play a vital role in upholding these standards, developing and implementing policies, monitoring compliance, and fostering an ethical culture within their institutions. By addressing the challenges and complexities of legal and ethical compliance, managers can contribute to the delivery of high-quality, patient-centred care.

In the next chapter, we will explore healthcare marketing and public relations. We will discuss strategies for effectively communicating with patients and the community, building the hospital's brand, and managing public perception. This will include practical insights into leveraging digital marketing, social media, and community engagement to enhance the hospital's reputation and reach.

CHAPTER 10: CRISIS AND RISK MANAGEMENT

Crisis and risk management are critical components of healthcare management, essential for ensuring patient safety, operational continuity, and the overall resilience of healthcare organisations. This chapter delves into the principles, strategies, and best practices for effective crisis and risk management in hospitals, highlighting the role of hospital managers in mitigating risks and responding to crises.

Understanding Crisis and Risk Management

Crisis and risk management in healthcare involve the identification, assessment, and prioritisation of risks, followed by the coordinated application of resources to minimise, monitor, and control the probability or impact of adverse events.

Definitions

- **Risk Management**: The systematic process of identifying, assessing, and addressing potential risks to prevent adverse outcomes and ensure safety and stability.
- **Crisis Management**: The process of preparing for, responding to, and recovering from emergencies or unexpected events that disrupt normal operations and threaten patient safety or organisational integrity.

Key Principles of Risk Management

Effective risk management in healthcare is based on several key principles:

Proactive Identification

1. **Risk Assessment**: Regularly conduct comprehensive risk assessments to identify potential hazards, vulnerabilities, and the likelihood of various adverse events.
2. **Risk Register**: Maintain a risk register those documents identified risks, their potential impact, and mitigation strategies.

Prevention and Mitigation

1. **Policy Development**: Develop and implement policies and procedures aimed at preventing risks and mitigating their impact.
2. **Training and Education**: Provide ongoing training and education to staff on risk management practices, emergency procedures, and safety protocols.

Continuous Monitoring

1. **Surveillance Systems**: Establish systems for continuous monitoring of risks, including incident reporting mechanisms and safety audits.
2. **Data Analysis**: Regularly analyse data on incidents and near-misses to identify trends and areas for improvement.

Response and Recovery

1. **Emergency Preparedness**: Develop and maintain emergency preparedness plans, including clear roles and responsibilities, communication strategies, and resource allocation.
2. **Recovery Plans**: Create recovery plans to ensure swift and effective recovery from crises, minimising disruption and restoring normal operations as quickly as possible.

Crisis Management Strategies

Crisis management involves a structured approach to dealing with emergencies and unexpected events. Effective strategies include:

Crisis Planning

1. **Risk Analysis**: Conduct thorough risk analysis to identify potential crises, such as natural disasters, pandemics, cyber-attacks, and system failures.
2. **Crisis Management Plan**: Develop a comprehensive crisis management plan that outlines specific actions to be taken before, during, and after a crisis. This plan should include:

   - **Communication Protocols**: Clear guidelines for internal and external communication during a crisis.

- **Resource Allocation**: Plans for mobilising and allocating resources, including personnel, equipment, and supplies.
- **Evacuation Procedures**: Detailed evacuation plans for patients, staff, and visitors if necessary.

Training and Drills

1. **Simulations and Drills**: Regularly conduct simulations and drills to test the effectiveness of the crisis management plan and ensure staff are familiar with their roles and responsibilities.
2. **Training Programs**: Provide comprehensive training programs on crisis management, emergency response, and incident command systems.

Communication

1. **Crisis Communication Team**: Establish a crisis communication team responsible for managing communication during a crisis, ensuring timely and accurate information dissemination.
2. **Stakeholder Engagement**: Engage with key stakeholders, including patients, families, staff, media, and the community, to maintain transparency and trust during a crisis.

The Role of Hospital Managers in Crisis and Risk Management

Hospital managers play a crucial role in crisis and risk management, ensuring that their organisations are prepared for, can respond to, and recover from crises effectively. Key responsibilities include:

Leadership and Coordination

1. **Leading the Response**: Provide strong leadership during crises, coordinating efforts, making critical decisions, and ensuring clear communication.
2. **Interdisciplinary Coordination**: Coordinate efforts across various departments and disciplines to ensure a unified and effective response.

Resource Management

1. **Resource Allocation**: Ensure that necessary resources, such as personnel, equipment, and supplies, are available and effectively utilised during a crisis.
2. **Financial Planning**: Plan for financial contingencies to support crisis response and recovery efforts.

Policy and Procedure Development

1. **Developing Policies**: Create and implement policies and procedures that support effective risk and crisis management.
2. **Review and Revision**: Regularly review and revise policies and procedures based on lessons learned from past incidents and emerging best practices.

Continuous Improvement

1. **Post-Crisis Evaluation**: Conduct thorough evaluations after crises to identify strengths, weaknesses, and areas for improvement.
2. **Incorporating Feedback**: Use feedback from staff, patients, and stakeholders to refine crisis management plans and enhance preparedness.

Challenges in Crisis and Risk Management

Despite best efforts, hospital managers may face several challenges in crisis and risk management, including:

Unpredictability of Crises

1. **Unexpected Events**: The unpredictable nature of crises can make it difficult to anticipate all potential scenarios and prepare accordingly.
2. **Rapid Changes**: Crises often evolve rapidly, requiring quick decision-making and adaptability.

Resource Constraints

1. **Limited Resources**: Resource limitations can hinder the ability to respond effectively to crises and manage risks.
2. **Competing Priorities**: Balancing crisis management with other organisational priorities can be challenging.

Communication Barriers

1. **Information Overload**: During crises, the influx of information can be overwhelming, making it difficult to disseminate clear and accurate messages.
2. **Stakeholder Coordination**: Coordinating communication and actions among diverse stakeholders can be complex.

Conclusion

Effective crisis and risk management are essential for ensuring patient safety, operational continuity, and the resilience of healthcare organisations. Hospital managers play a pivotal role in developing and implementing strategies to identify, assess, and mitigate risks, as well as preparing for and responding to crises. By fostering a culture of preparedness, continuous improvement, and proactive risk management, hospital managers can enhance their organisations' ability to navigate challenges and maintain high standards of care.

In the next chapter, we will explore healthcare marketing and public relations. We will discuss strategies for effectively communicating with patients and the community, building the hospital's brand, and managing public perception. This will include practical insights into leveraging digital marketing, social media, and community engagement to enhance the hospital's reputation and reach.

CHAPTER 11: INNOVATIONS IN HEALTHCARE DELIVERY

Innovations in healthcare delivery are transforming the landscape of medical care, enhancing patient outcomes, increasing efficiency, and improving accessibility. This chapter explores various innovations that are revolutionising healthcare delivery, the impact of these advancements, and the role of hospital managers in fostering and integrating innovation within their organisations.

Telemedicine and Telehealth

Telemedicine and telehealth have emerged as pivotal innovations, enabling remote diagnosis, treatment, and patient monitoring. These technologies bridge the gap between patients and healthcare providers, particularly in rural and underserved areas.

Benefits of Telemedicine

1. **Accessibility**: Telemedicine increases access to healthcare services, allowing patients in remote locations to consult with specialists without the need for travel.
2. **Convenience**: Patients can receive medical advice and follow-up care from the comfort of their homes.

3. **Cost-Effectiveness**: Reduces healthcare costs by minimising the need for in-person visits and hospital admissions.
4. **Continuity of Care**: Enhances continuity of care through regular virtual follow-ups and remote monitoring.

Applications of Telemedicine

1. **Remote Consultations**: Virtual consultations with doctors and specialists for diagnosis, treatment plans, and follow-ups.
2. **Chronic Disease Management**: Remote monitoring and management of chronic conditions such as diabetes, hypertension, and heart disease.
3. **Mental Health Services**: Access to counselling and therapy sessions through telepsychiatry and telepsychology.
4. **Emergency Care**: Tele-triage systems to assess and manage emergencies remotely, directing patients to appropriate care settings.

Artificial Intelligence (AI) and Machine Learning

AI and machine learning are transforming healthcare delivery by enabling data-driven decision-making, predictive analytics, and personalised medicine.

Applications of AI in Healthcare

1. **Diagnostic Imaging**: AI algorithms assist in interpreting medical images, identifying abnormalities, and aiding radiologists in diagnosing conditions such as cancer and cardiovascular diseases.
2. **Predictive Analytics**: AI models analyse patient data to predict disease outbreaks, patient deterioration, and readmission risks, allowing for proactive interventions.
3. **Personalised Medicine**: Machine learning algorithms analyse genetic, clinical, and lifestyle data to tailor treatments to individual patients.

4. **Administrative Efficiency**: AI streamlines administrative tasks such as scheduling, billing, and patient record management, reducing operational burdens.

Robotics and Automation

Robotics and automation are enhancing the precision and efficiency of surgical procedures, rehabilitation, and routine tasks within healthcare settings.

Robotics in Surgery

1. **Minimally Invasive Procedures**: Robotic-assisted surgery allows for minimally invasive procedures with greater precision, reduced recovery times, and fewer complications.
2. **Complex Surgeries**: Robots assist in performing complex surgeries that require high levels of dexterity and precision.

Automation in Healthcare

1. **Medication Dispensing**: Automated medication dispensing systems reduce the risk of errors and ensure timely administration of medications.
2. **Laboratory Automation**: Automated laboratory systems improve the accuracy and efficiency of diagnostic testing and sample processing.
3. **Patient Care**: Robotic systems assist in patient care tasks such as lifting, mobility support, and rehabilitation exercises.

Wearable Health Technology

Wearable health devices are empowering patients to monitor their health and manage chronic conditions more effectively.

Types of Wearable Devices

1. **Fitness Trackers**: Devices that monitor physical activity, heart rate, sleep patterns, and overall fitness levels.
2. **Medical Wearables**: Devices that track vital signs such as blood pressure, glucose levels, and ECG, providing real-time health data to patients and healthcare providers.
3. **Rehabilitation Wearables**: Wearable devices that support rehabilitation exercises and monitor progress in real-time.

Benefits of Wearable Technology

1. **Patient Engagement**: Encourages patients to take an active role in managing their health and wellness.
2. **Early Detection**: Enables early detection of potential health issues through continuous monitoring.
3. **Data-Driven Insights**: Provides healthcare providers with valuable data for personalised treatment plans and proactive interventions.

Genomics and Precision Medicine

Advances in genomics and precision medicine are enabling more accurate diagnoses and targeted treatments based on individual genetic profiles.

Genomic Innovations

1. **Genetic Testing**: Identifies genetic predispositions to diseases, allowing for early interventions and personalised preventive measures.
2. **Pharmacogenomics**: Tailors drug therapies based on genetic profiles to optimise efficacy and minimise adverse effects.

Precision Medicine

1. **Targeted Therapies**: Develops treatments that specifically target genetic mutations or molecular pathways involved in diseases such as cancer.
2. **Personalised Treatment Plans**: Combines genetic, clinical, and lifestyle data to create customised treatment plans for individual patients.

Integrating Innovations into Healthcare Delivery

The successful integration of innovations in healthcare delivery requires strategic planning, investment, and a culture of continuous improvement.

Role of Hospital Managers

1. **Strategic Vision**: Develop a strategic vision that incorporates technological advancements and fosters a culture of innovation.
2. **Investment in Technology**: Allocate resources for the adoption and implementation of new technologies, ensuring that the necessary infrastructure and training are in place.
3. **Collaboration and Partnerships**: Collaborate with technology providers, research institutions, and other healthcare organisations to stay abreast of emerging innovations and best practices.
4. **Training and Education**: Provide ongoing training and education for staff to ensure they are proficient in using new technologies and understand their benefits and limitations.
5. **Patient-Centred Approach**: Engage patients in the adoption of new technologies, educating them on the benefits and ensuring their needs and preferences are considered.

Overcoming Challenges

1. **Cost and Budget Constraints**: Address cost and budget constraints by prioritising investments in technologies that offer the greatest potential for improving patient outcomes and operational efficiency.

2. **Regulatory Compliance**: Ensure compliance with regulatory requirements and standards when adopting new technologies, particularly those related to patient safety and data security.
3. **Change Management**: Implement effective change management strategies to address resistance and ensure smooth transitions to new systems and processes.

Conclusion

Innovations in healthcare delivery are reshaping the way care is provided, offering new opportunities for improving patient outcomes, enhancing operational efficiency, and increasing accessibility. Hospital managers play a crucial role in driving and managing these innovations, ensuring that their organisations remain at the forefront of technological advancements and continue to deliver high-quality, patient-centred care.

In the next chapter, we will explore healthcare marketing and public relations. We will discuss strategies for effectively communicating with patients and the community, building the hospital's brand, and managing public perception. This will include practical insights into leveraging digital marketing, social media, and community engagement to enhance the hospital's reputation and reach.

CHAPTER 12: COMMUNITY AND PUBLIC HEALTH RELATIONS

Effective community and public health relations are essential for building trust, fostering collaboration, and promoting health and well-being within the community. This chapter explores strategies for engaging with the community, enhancing public health initiatives, and building a strong hospital brand through effective communication and public relations.

The Importance of Community and Public Health Relations

Engaging with the community and establishing strong public health relations provide several benefits for hospitals and healthcare organisations:

1. **Trust and Credibility**: Building trust and credibility with the community enhances the hospital's reputation and fosters loyalty among patients and stakeholders.
2. **Community Health Improvement**: Collaborative public health initiatives can lead to improved health outcomes and reduced healthcare disparities.
3. **Patient Engagement**: Active community engagement promotes patient involvement in their own health and encourages the use of hospital services.
4. **Support for Hospital Initiatives**: Community support is vital for the success of hospital initiatives, including fundraising efforts and public health campaigns.

Strategies for Effective Community Engagement

Building Relationships with Community Leaders

1. **Identify Key Stakeholders**: Identify and establish relationships with key community leaders, including local

government officials, religious leaders, business owners, and community organisations.
2. **Regular Communication**: Maintain regular communication with community leaders to keep them informed about hospital initiatives, events, and developments.
3. **Collaborative Projects**: Partner with community leaders on collaborative projects that address local health needs and priorities.

Community Outreach and Education

1. **Health Education Programmes**: Organise health education programmes, workshops, and seminars to inform the community about preventive care, chronic disease management, and healthy lifestyle choices.
2. **School Partnerships**: Partner with local schools to provide health education and screenings for students, parents, and teachers.
3. **Public Health Campaigns**: Launch public health campaigns on topics such as vaccination, nutrition, mental health, and substance abuse prevention.

Volunteering and Service Initiatives

1. **Volunteer Programmes**: Develop volunteer programmes that encourage hospital staff and community members to participate in service initiatives and community outreach activities.
2. **Health Fairs and Screenings**: Organise health fairs and free health screenings in collaboration with community organisations to increase access to healthcare services.
3. **Support Groups**: Facilitate support groups for patients and caregivers dealing with chronic conditions, mental health issues, or specific health challenges.

Enhancing Public Health Initiatives

Collaborative Public Health Efforts

1. **Public-Private Partnerships**: Establish public-private partnerships to address community health issues, leveraging resources and expertise from both sectors.
2. **Joint Research and Data Sharing**: Collaborate with local health departments, academic institutions, and other healthcare providers on research projects and data sharing to better understand and address public health needs.
3. **Emergency Preparedness**: Work with community organisations and local authorities to develop and implement emergency preparedness plans, ensuring coordinated responses to public health emergencies.

Targeted Health Interventions

1. **Community Health Needs Assessments**: Conduct regular community health needs assessments to identify priority health issues and target interventions where they are most needed.
2. **Health Promotion and Disease Prevention**: Implement targeted health promotion and disease prevention programmes, focusing on areas such as immunisation, maternal and child health, and chronic disease management.
3. **Addressing Social Determinants of Health**: Develop initiatives to address social determinants of health, such as housing, education, and employment, which impact community health outcomes.

Building a Strong Hospital Brand

Effective Communication Strategies

1. **Transparent Communication**: Ensure transparent and honest communication with the community, sharing both successes and challenges.
2. **Consistent Messaging**: Maintain consistent messaging across all communication channels to reinforce the hospital's mission, values, and commitment to quality care.

3. **Utilising Multiple Channels**: Use a variety of communication channels, including social media, newsletters, websites, and community events, to reach diverse audiences.

Media Relations

1. **Proactive Media Engagement**: Build positive relationships with local media by providing regular updates, press releases, and access to hospital experts for interviews.
2. **Crisis Communication**: Develop and implement a crisis communication plan to manage and respond to negative publicity or emergencies effectively.
3. **Highlighting Success Stories**: Share success stories, patient testimonials, and case studies to showcase the hospital's impact on individual lives and the community.

Community Involvement in Decision-Making

1. **Advisory Boards and Committees**: Establish community advisory boards and committees to involve community members in decision-making processes and gather feedback on hospital services and initiatives.
2. **Patient and Family Councils**: Create patient and family councils to engage patients and their families in discussions about hospital policies, programmes, and quality improvement efforts.
3. **Public Forums and Town Hall Meetings**: Organise public forums and town hall meetings to provide updates on hospital activities, gather community input, and address concerns.

Evaluating Community and Public Health Relations Efforts

Measuring Impact

1. **Key Performance Indicators (KPIs)**: Develop and track key performance indicators (KPIs) to measure the

effectiveness of community engagement and public health initiatives.
2. **Community Surveys and Feedback**: Conduct regular surveys and gather feedback from community members to assess their perceptions of the hospital and its services.
3. **Health Outcomes**: Monitor health outcomes and public health data to evaluate the impact of targeted health interventions and community health programmes.

Continuous Improvement

1. **Regular Review and Analysis**: Regularly review and analyse community engagement efforts and public health initiatives to identify strengths, weaknesses, and areas for improvement.
2. **Incorporating Feedback**: Use feedback from community members, patients, and stakeholders to refine strategies and enhance the effectiveness of programmes.
3. **Adapting to Changing Needs**: Stay attuned to changing community needs and priorities, adapting initiatives and communication strategies accordingly.

Conclusion

Effective community and public health relations are essential for building trust, fostering collaboration, and promoting health and well-being within the community. Hospital managers play a vital role in developing and implementing strategies that engage the community, enhance public health initiatives, and build a strong hospital brand. By prioritising transparent communication, collaboration, and continuous improvement, hospitals can create meaningful connections with the community and contribute to better health outcomes.

In the next chapter, we will explore healthcare marketing and public relations. We will discuss strategies for effectively communicating with patients and the community, building the hospital's brand, and managing public perception. This will include practical insights into leveraging digital marketing, social media, and community engagement to enhance the hospital's reputation and reach.

CHAPTER 13: PATIENT EXPERIENCE AND SATISFACTION

Patient experience and satisfaction are critical indicators of the quality of care provided by hospitals and healthcare organisations. This chapter explores the key elements that contribute to a positive patient experience, strategies for measuring and improving patient satisfaction, and the role of hospital managers in fostering a patient-centred culture.

Understanding Patient Experience and Satisfaction

Definitions

1. **Patient Experience**: Encompasses all interactions that patients have with the healthcare system, including care from health plans, doctors, nurses, and staff in hospitals, physician practices, and other healthcare facilities.
2. **Patient Satisfaction**: A measure of how well patients' expectations about a health encounter are met. It reflects the overall perception of care and services received.

Importance of Patient Experience and Satisfaction

1. **Quality of Care**: Positive patient experiences are closely linked to high-quality care and better health outcomes.
2. **Reputation and Trust**: Hospitals that provide excellent patient experiences build strong reputations and gain trust within the community.
3. **Patient Loyalty**: Satisfied patients are more likely to return for future care and recommend the hospital to others.

4. **Financial Performance**: Higher patient satisfaction can lead to better financial performance through increased patient retention and reimbursements tied to patient experience metrics.

Key Elements of a Positive Patient Experience

Effective Communication

1. **Clear Information**: Providing clear, comprehensive information about diagnoses, treatments, and procedures helps patients make informed decisions.
2. **Empathy and Compassion**: Healthcare providers who listen attentively and show empathy and compassion create a supportive and caring environment.
3. **Language and Cultural Sensitivity**: Ensuring communication is respectful of patients' cultural backgrounds and language preferences enhances their comfort and understanding.

Timely and Efficient Care

1. **Reduced Waiting Times**: Minimising waiting times for appointments, tests, and procedures improves patient satisfaction.
2. **Streamlined Processes**: Efficient administrative processes, such as registration and billing, reduce patient frustration and enhance their overall experience.
3. **Coordination of Care**: Coordinating care across different providers and settings ensures seamless transitions and continuity of care.

Comfortable and Safe Environment

1. **Clean and Safe Facilities**: Maintaining clean, safe, and comfortable facilities promotes patient well-being and confidence in the hospital.

2. **Privacy and Dignity**: Respecting patients' privacy and dignity during examinations, treatments, and interactions is essential.

3. **Support Services**: Providing support services, such as chaplaincy, social work, and patient advocacy, addresses patients' emotional and social needs.

Patient Involvement and Empowerment

1. **Shared Decision-Making**: Involving patients in decision-making about their care plans fosters a sense of control and partnership.

2. **Education and Resources**: Offering education and resources about managing health conditions empowers patients to take an active role in their care.

3. **Feedback Mechanisms**: Encouraging and valuing patient feedback helps identify areas for improvement and demonstrates a commitment to patient-centred care.

Measuring Patient Satisfaction

Survey Tools

1. **CAHPS Surveys**: The Consumer Assessment of Healthcare Providers and Systems (CAHPS) surveys are standardised tools for measuring patient experiences in various healthcare settings.

(CAHPS (Consumer Assessment of Healthcare Providers and Systems) surveys are a set of standardised tools used to measure patients' experiences with healthcare providers and systems. Developed and maintained by the Agency for Healthcare Research and Quality (AHRQ) in the United States, CAHPS surveys are widely recognised and utilised globally to assess the quality of care from the patient's perspective. This chapter explores the purpose, methodology, and applications of CAHPS surveys, as well as their importance in improving healthcare delivery.)

2. **Press Ganey Surveys**: Press Ganey provides comprehensive patient satisfaction surveys that cover a wide range of aspects related to patient care and experience.

3. **In-House Surveys**: Customised in-house surveys tailored to specific hospital needs can provide valuable insights into patient satisfaction.

Key Performance Indicators (KPIs)

1. **Overall Satisfaction Scores**: Measuring overall satisfaction with the hospital and specific departments provides a broad view of patient experiences.
2. **Net Promoter Score (NPS)**: NPS measures the likelihood of patients recommending the hospital to others, indicating their overall satisfaction and loyalty.
3. **Patient Complaints and Compliments**: Tracking and analysing patient complaints and compliments helps identify patterns and areas for improvement.

Strategies for Improving Patient Experience and Satisfaction

Enhancing Communication and Interaction

1. **Communication Training**: Providing training for healthcare providers in effective communication, empathy, and cultural competence.
2. **Patient Rounding**: Regular rounding by nurses and doctors to check on patients, address concerns, and provide updates on care plans.
3. **Technology Solutions**: Implementing technology solutions, such as patient portals and telehealth, to facilitate communication and access to information.

Improving Operational Efficiency

1. **Lean Processes**: Adopting lean processes to eliminate waste, streamline workflows, and improve efficiency in patient care and administrative tasks.

2. **Appointment Scheduling**: Optimising appointment scheduling systems to reduce wait times and enhance the patient flow.
3. **Electronic Health Records (EHR)**: Utilizing EHR systems to improve coordination, reduce errors, and provide timely access to patient information.

Fostering a Patient-Centred Culture

1. **Leadership Commitment**: Hospital leadership must demonstrate a commitment to patient-centred care through policies, practices, and resource allocation.
2. **Staff Engagement**: Engaging staff at all levels in efforts to improve patient experience and recognising their contributions.
3. **Patient Advisory Councils**: Establishing patient advisory councils to provide input on hospital policies, services, and improvement initiatives.

The Role of Hospital Managers

Leading by Example

1. **Vision and Mission**: Articulating a clear vision and mission that prioritises patient experience and satisfaction.
2. **Visibility and Accessibility**: Being visible and accessible to staff, patients, and families to understand their needs and concerns.

Resource Allocation

1. **Investing in Training**: Allocating resources for staff training and development in areas such as communication, cultural competence, and patient-centred care.
2. **Technology and Infrastructure**: Investing in technology and infrastructure improvements that enhance the patient experience.

Monitoring and Evaluation

1. **Regular Assessments**: Conducting regular assessments of patient satisfaction and experience using surveys, focus groups, and feedback mechanisms.
2. **Continuous Improvement**: Implementing continuous improvement initiatives based on patient feedback and satisfaction data.

Challenges in Enhancing Patient Experience

Resource Constraints

1. **Budget Limitations**: Limited financial resources can impact the ability to invest in new technologies, staff training, and facility upgrades.
2. **Staffing Issues**: Staffing shortages and high turnover rates can affect the consistency and quality of patient care.

Balancing Competing Priorities

1. **Operational Demands**: Balancing the need to improve patient experience with other operational demands and financial pressures.
2. **Regulatory Compliance**: Ensuring compliance with regulatory requirements while striving to enhance patient satisfaction.

Conclusion

Improving patient experience and satisfaction is essential for delivering high-quality, patient-centred care. Hospital managers play a crucial role in fostering a culture that prioritises patient needs, enhancing communication and operational efficiency, and continuously monitoring and improving patient satisfaction. By addressing challenges and implementing effective strategies, hospitals can create positive, meaningful experiences for their patients, leading to better health outcomes, increased patient loyalty, and a stronger reputation within the community.

In the next chapter, we will explore healthcare marketing and public relations. We will discuss strategies for effectively communicating with patients and the community, building the hospital's brand, and managing public perception. This will include practical insights into leveraging digital marketing, social media, and community engagement to enhance the hospital's reputation and reach.

CHAPTER 14: FUTURE TRENDS IN HOSPITAL MANAGEMENT

The healthcare industry is rapidly evolving, driven by technological advancements, changing patient expectations, and global health challenges. Hospital management must adapt to these changes to ensure sustainable and high-quality care. This chapter explores the future trends in hospital management, focusing on innovations, emerging practices, and strategic shifts that will shape the future of healthcare.

Technological Advancements

Artificial Intelligence and Machine Learning

1. **Enhanced Diagnostics**: AI and machine learning algorithms can analyse medical images and patient data to improve diagnostic accuracy and speed.
2. **Predictive Analytics**: AI-driven predictive analytics can forecast patient outcomes, identify at-risk populations, and optimise resource allocation.
3. **Personalised Treatment Plans**: Machine learning models can tailor treatment plans based on individual patient profiles, improving outcomes and reducing adverse effects.

Telemedicine and Telehealth

1. **Remote Consultations**: The adoption of telemedicine will continue to grow, providing remote access to healthcare services, especially in rural and underserved areas.
2. **Chronic Disease Management**: Telehealth platforms will enhance the management of chronic diseases through regular monitoring and virtual follow-ups.
3. **Virtual Care Teams**: Multi-disciplinary virtual care teams will collaborate remotely to provide comprehensive care to patients.

Robotics and Automation

1. **Robotic Surgery**: Advancements in robotic surgery will increase precision, reduce recovery times, and lower the risk of complications.
2. **Automated Workflows**: Automation of administrative and clinical workflows will streamline operations, reduce errors, and improve efficiency.
3. **Robotic Assistance in Patient Care**: Robots will assist in patient care tasks such as lifting, mobility support, and rehabilitation.

Patient-Centred Care

Personalised Medicine

1. **Genomics and Biomarker Research**: Advances in genomics and biomarker research will enable more precise and personalised treatments for a variety of conditions.
2. **Tailored Therapies**: Personalised medicine will shift from a one-size-fits-all approach to treatments tailored to the genetic and molecular profiles of patients.

Patient Engagement and Empowerment

1. **Health Apps and Wearables**: The use of health apps and wearable devices will empower patients to monitor their health and engage in self-care.
2. **Patient Portals**: Enhanced patient portals will provide access to medical records, appointment scheduling, and direct communication with healthcare providers.
3. **Shared Decision-Making**: Greater emphasis on shared decision-making will involve patients more actively in their care plans, improving satisfaction and outcomes.

Workforce Development

Continuous Education and Training

1. **Upskilling Healthcare Professionals**: Continuous education and training programmes will be essential to keep healthcare professionals updated with the latest advancements and practices.
2. **Interdisciplinary Training**: Interdisciplinary training will promote collaboration among different healthcare professionals, enhancing team-based care.

Workforce Well-being

1. **Burnout Prevention**: Strategies to prevent burnout, such as mental health support and flexible working conditions, will be crucial for maintaining a healthy and motivated workforce.

2. **Work-Life Balance**: Hospitals will adopt policies that promote work-life balance, reducing stress and improving job satisfaction among staff.

Sustainability and Environmental Responsibility

Green Hospital Initiatives

1. **Energy Efficiency**: Hospitals will invest in energy-efficient technologies and renewable energy sources to reduce their environmental footprint.
2. **Waste Management**: Improved waste management practices, including recycling and safe disposal of medical waste, will be prioritised.
3. **Sustainable Building Design**: New hospital constructions and renovations will focus on sustainable building designs that promote energy conservation and environmental sustainability.

Community Health and Social Responsibility

1. **Population Health Management**: Hospitals will adopt population health management strategies to address social determinants of health and improve community well-being.
2. **Community Partnerships**: Collaborations with community organisations and public health agencies will enhance the delivery of comprehensive healthcare services.
3. **Health Equity**: Efforts to address health disparities and promote health equity will be integral to hospital management strategies.

Data-Driven Decision Making

Big Data and Analytics

1. **Clinical Decision Support**: Big data analytics will support clinical decision-making by providing insights into patient outcomes, treatment efficacy, and healthcare trends.

2. **Operational Efficiency**: Data analytics will optimise hospital operations, from resource allocation to supply chain management.
3. **Predictive Modelling**: Predictive modelling will enhance the ability to anticipate patient needs, manage risks, and improve overall hospital performance.

Cybersecurity

1. **Data Protection**: As hospitals become increasingly digital, robust cybersecurity measures will be essential to protect patient data and maintain trust.
2. **Incident Response**: Developing and implementing effective incident response plans will help mitigate the impact of cyberattacks and data breaches.
3. **Compliance with Regulations**: Ensuring compliance with data protection regulations, such as GDPR and HIPAA, will be a priority for hospital management.

Innovative Care Models

Value-Based Care

1. **Outcome-Based Reimbursement**: Transitioning to value-based care models that reward outcomes rather than volume will incentivise quality care and cost efficiency.
2. **Integrated Care Pathways**: Developing integrated care pathways that coordinate services across different providers and settings will enhance patient care continuity.

Home Healthcare

1. **Hospital-at-Home**: Expanding hospital-at-home programmes will allow patients to receive acute care in the comfort of their homes, reducing hospital admissions and costs.
2. **Remote Monitoring**: Advanced remote monitoring technologies will support home healthcare, providing real-time data to healthcare providers and enabling timely interventions.

Community-Based Healthcare

1. **Mobile Health Clinics**: Deploying mobile health clinics will bring healthcare services to underserved communities, improving access to care.
2. **Community Health Workers**: Training and employing community health workers will strengthen the connection between hospitals and the communities they serve.

Conclusion

The future of hospital management will be shaped by technological innovations, a focus on patient-centred care, workforce development, sustainability, data-driven decision making, and innovative care models. Hospital managers must stay abreast of these trends and adapt their strategies to meet the evolving needs of patients, staff, and the community. By embracing change and fostering a culture of continuous improvement, hospitals can ensure the delivery of high-quality, efficient, and equitable healthcare in the years to come.

In the next chapter, we will delve into healthcare marketing and public relations. We will discuss strategies for effectively communicating with patients and the community, building the hospital's brand, and managing public perception. This will include practical insights into leveraging digital marketing, social media, and community engagement to enhance the hospital's reputation and reach.

CHAPTER 15: CASE STUDIES AND BEST PRACTICES

Examining real-world examples and best practices in hospital management offers valuable insights into the strategies and approaches that lead to successful outcomes. This chapter presents case studies from various hospitals, highlighting their innovative practices, challenges faced, and the lessons learned. These case studies illustrate how hospitals can implement best practices in different areas of management to improve patient care, operational efficiency, and overall performance.

Case Study 1: Enhancing Patient Experience at Cleveland Clinic

Background

Cleveland Clinic, a renowned healthcare institution in the United States, recognised the need to enhance patient experience to maintain its reputation for excellence in care. The hospital aimed to create a patient-centred culture by focusing on empathy, communication, and continuous improvement.

Strategies Implemented

1. **Empathy Training**: Cleveland Clinic introduced empathy training programmes for all staff members, including doctors, nurses, and administrative personnel. The training emphasised active listening, compassionate communication, and emotional support for patients and their families.
2. **Patient Rounding**: The hospital implemented regular patient rounding by nurses and doctors. During these rounds,

healthcare providers checked on patients, addressed their concerns, and provided updates on their care plans.

3. **Patient Advisory Councils**: Cleveland Clinic established patient advisory councils to involve patients and their families in decision-making processes. These councils provided feedback on hospital policies, services, and improvement initiatives.

4. **Feedback Mechanisms**: The hospital utilised various feedback mechanisms, including surveys and focus groups, to gather insights from patients about their experiences. This feedback was used to identify areas for improvement and implement changes.

Outcomes

- **Improved Patient Satisfaction**: The initiatives led to a significant increase in patient satisfaction scores. Patients reported feeling more valued and respected, and their overall experience at the hospital improved.
- **Enhanced Staff Engagement**: The focus on empathy and patient-centred care fostered a more positive and supportive work environment for staff, leading to higher levels of engagement and job satisfaction.
- **Reputation and Trust**: Cleveland Clinic's commitment to patient experience strengthened its reputation and trust within the community, attracting more patients and enhancing loyalty.

Case Study 2: Implementing Lean Processes at Virginia Mason Medical Centre

Background

Virginia Mason Medical Centre in Seattle, Washington, aimed to improve operational efficiency and reduce waste by implementing lean management principles. The hospital sought to streamline workflows, enhance patient care, and reduce costs.

Strategies Implemented

1. **Lean Training**: Virginia Mason provided extensive lean training to staff at all levels, including executives, managers, and frontline workers. The training focused on identifying and eliminating waste, standardising processes, and continuous improvement.
2. **Value Stream Mapping**: The hospital conducted value stream mapping exercises to analyse and redesign key processes, such as patient admission, discharge, and surgical procedures. This helped identify inefficiencies and areas for improvement.
3. **Kaizen Events**: Virginia Mason organised regular Kaizen events, which are focused, team-based improvement projects. These events addressed specific issues, such as reducing wait times in the emergency department or improving the efficiency of the operating room.
4. **Visual Management**: The hospital implemented visual management tools, such as performance boards and dashboards, to track key performance indicators (KPIs) and monitor progress towards goals.

Outcomes

- **Reduced Wait Times**: The lean initiatives led to significant reductions in patient wait times for various services, including emergency care and surgeries.
- **Cost Savings**: By eliminating waste and optimising processes, Virginia Mason achieved substantial cost savings, which were reinvested in patient care and facility improvements.
- **Higher Quality Care**: The focus on continuous improvement and standardised processes enhanced the quality and consistency of patient care.

Case Study 3: Advancing Telehealth Services at Kaiser Permanente

Background

Kaiser Permanente, one of the largest integrated healthcare systems in the United States, sought to expand its telehealth services to improve access to care and enhance patient convenience. The goal was to provide high-quality, remote healthcare services to patients across its extensive network.

Strategies Implemented

1. **Telehealth Infrastructure**: Kaiser Permanente invested in robust telehealth infrastructure, including secure video conferencing platforms, electronic health records (EHR) integration, and remote monitoring tools.
2. **Training and Support**: The organisation provided comprehensive training for healthcare providers on how to conduct effective telehealth consultations. Support teams were established to assist both patients and providers with technical issues.
3. **Patient Education**: Kaiser Permanente launched educational campaigns to inform patients about the availability and benefits of telehealth services. This included instructional videos, online resources, and in-person workshops.
4. **Expansion of Services**: The range of telehealth services was expanded to include primary care, specialist consultations, mental health services, and chronic disease management. Virtual care teams were created to provide coordinated and comprehensive care.

Outcomes

- **Increased Access to Care**: Telehealth services significantly increased access to care, especially for patients in rural or underserved areas. Patients were able to receive timely consultations without the need for travel.
- **High Patient Satisfaction**: Patient satisfaction with telehealth services was high, with many patients appreciating the convenience and efficiency of remote consultations.

- **Improved Health Outcomes**: The ability to monitor and manage chronic conditions remotely led to better health outcomes for patients, with improved adherence to treatment plans and reduced hospital admissions.

Best Practices in Hospital Management

Patient-Centred Care

1. **Empathy and Communication**: Training healthcare providers in empathy and effective communication enhances patient experience and satisfaction.
2. **Involving Patients and Families**: Engaging patients and their families in decision-making processes fosters a sense of partnership and trust.

Operational Efficiency

1. **Lean Management**: Implementing lean principles helps streamline workflows, reduce waste, and improve operational efficiency.
2. **Data-Driven Decision Making**: Utilising data analytics to inform decision-making processes ensures that resources are allocated effectively and performance is optimised.

Technology Integration

1. **Telehealth Services**: Expanding telehealth services increases access to care and enhances patient convenience.
2. **Electronic Health Records**: Integrating EHR systems improves coordination of care, reduces errors, and provides timely access to patient information.

Workforce Development

1. **Continuous Training**: Providing ongoing training and development opportunities for staff ensures they remain updated with the latest advancements and best practices.

2. **Supportive Work Environment**: Creating a supportive work environment that addresses staff well-being and promotes work-life balance enhances job satisfaction and retention.

Conclusion

Case studies and best practices provide valuable lessons for hospital managers seeking to improve patient care, operational efficiency, and overall performance. By examining successful strategies and learning from real-world examples, hospital managers can implement effective practices that lead to better outcomes for patients, staff, and the organisation as a whole. The continuous pursuit of excellence and innovation is essential for navigating the evolving healthcare landscape and delivering high-quality, patient-centred care.

In the next chapter, we will summarise the key points covered in this book and provide actionable recommendations for hospital managers looking to apply these insights to their own organisations. This will include practical tips and strategies for implementing best practices, overcoming challenges, and driving continuous improvement in hospital management.

www.ingramcontent.com/pod-product-compliance
Lightning Source LLC
Chambersburg PA
CBHW071946210526
45479CB00002B/829